Inspirational Poetry Book

given to

Susan Matheson-Bailey

by

God The Father

Inspirational POETRY BOOK

SUSAN MATHESON-BAILEY

Guardian
B O O K S

Belleville, Ontario, Canada

ISBN: 978-1-55452-131-9
LSI Edition: 978-1-4600-0567-5
E-book ISBN: 978-1-4600-0568-2

Cataloguing data available from Library and Archives Canada

To order additional copies, visit:
www.essencebookstore.com

Guardian Books is an imprint of *Essence Publishing,* a Christian Book Publisher dedicated to furthering the work of Christ through the written word. For more information, contact:
20 Hanna Court, Belleville, Ontario, Canada K8P 5J2
Phone: 1-800-238-6376 • Fax: (613) 962-3055
Email: info@essence-publishing.com
Web site: www.essence-publishing.com

Printed in Canada
by

Guardian
B O O K S

Table Of Contents

Acknowledgment

I would like to give thanks and a big shout-out to my Heavenly Father first and utmost. I really and truly want to thank Him for choosing me to do these projects. Thank You. Also, to all who inspire me in writing these poems, once again, thank you. Last but not least, to my publisher, I just want to say thank you. I thank God for everyone who had a part in the publication of this book. I pray that God richly blesses one and all.

Introduction

In this poetry book, you will see that the poems are about things that happen in everyday life. If you live in this society, I know you can understand the poems in this book.

Let us look at "What If?" Every day, every hour, every minute, every second, old people, young people and babies are being diagnosed with some kind of critical disease that doctors cannot cure. What would you do, and who would you turn to? In this case, there is only One you can turn to.

Let us take a look also at "Do Not Judge Me." In everyday life, people are judged by the way they are dressed, the hairstyles that they wear or their personal affairs. Having a child out of wedlock at a young age is not only judged by the people in the world but also by the people in the Church. So instead of judging, why don't we take that time and pray for each other?

I hope that as you read this poetry book, each and every poem will inspire you. You will notice that these poems are based on real-life situations and things that people think about every day. Also, you will notice how the Heavenly Father can work miraculously in a person's life. If you just turn to Him, all of your problems will be taken care of. I hope that through this poetry book, you will receive grace and encouragement. Just read along to be inspired and reflect on everyday life situations.

A MOTHER LIKE YOU...

mother like you
is what I always
wished for.
A mother like you
is what I prayed for.
A mother like you
is very special to me.
Having a mother like you,
what else do I need?
A mother who cares.
A mother who prays.
A mother who will wipe
my tears away.
A mother who is always
there, wondering if I am okay.
What more can I ask for?
God really answered my
prayers
When He blessed me with
a mother like you.

BELIEVE....

Believe in God's Word
and its wonder.
Believe that there's
sunshine behind every cloud.
Believe that miracles happen
each day.
Believe that each prayer is answered
by the grace of heaven above.
Believe that unsaved souls
will be saved.
Believe that God will bless
you abundantly.
Believe that God will make
that crooked way straight.
Believe that grace saves us.
Just stand strong and say,
"God, I believe in You..."

BLESSED

 lessed is the man who walks under the
shadow of the Almighty.
Blessed are the meek.
Blessed is the man who walks with humility.
Blessed is he who endureths the wrong and the right.
Blessed are the poor in spirit.
Blessed is he who has faith in God.
Blessed is the man or woman who is in distress and looks
solely to the Most High.
Blessed are the pure in heart.
Blessed is he who has favor in the Lord.
Blessed are the men who thirst for righteousness.
Blessed are the evildoers, for their days shall and will be
short in their upcoming.
Blessed are the men who trust in the Lord.
Blessed is the man who says there is no God
for he shall not see the light.
Blessed is the man who walks with his head upright.
Blessed is the man who helps his brother and sister in
time of need.
Blessed are the seekers and finders of the Holy Ghost.
Blessed are the believers of Christ.

Matthew 5:3-12

REJOICE

Rejoice in your pain.
Rejoice in your hurt.
Rejoice when you have and when you
don't.
Rejoice in your sorrows and your distress.
Rejoice when all manner of evil comes against you.
Rejoice when your bills are due and there are not enough
funds to pay them.
Rejoice when you are getting attacked from the north,
south, east and west.
Rejoice when they are slandering you behind your back.
Rejoice when your own family members turn their backs
on you.
Rejoice when you are sick.
Rejoice when you are going through tests and trials.
Rejoice through it all.

Philippians 4:4

BLINDED

Take a look and tell me,
What do you see?
Nothing, that is what you said to me.
Blinded by our own surroundings.
Blinded by our own actions.
Blinded by the things of this world.
Blinded, that is what we are.

Do you ever stop and think,
Why are all these things happening to me?
Sit back and think.
When we were doing the things that we had no business
doing,
We never thought to figure out why these things were hap-
pening to us.

That is what we are, "blinded."
We are not only blinded in the world
But we enter into the Kingdom with the
Same blindness.
Why do we do that? one might ask.
We are so used to the blindness that
It feels okay.
Walking with Christ, we walk into the light,
But walking with the defeated foe, we walk in darkness,
And that is when the blindness seeps in.

Blinded by vain images.
Blinded by worldly possessions.

BLINDED

Blinded by evil thoughts.
Blinded by principalities of this world.
Sit and think on this for at least a second
And answer this question:
Do You Want To Be Blinded For The Rest
Of Your Life?

CHANGES...

e have to go through a lot of changes in life.
Sometimes the changes are good.
Sometimes the changes are bad.
Sometimes the changes come to elevate us in life.
And sometimes changes bring us down.

One may ask: how do you handle the changes
that are going on in your life?
I can speak for myself.
I am going through a lot of changes in my life
right now. I am going through changes on my job.
I am going through changes in my home.
I am going through changes with my children.
I am going through changes with my spouse.
I am going through a lot of changes in my life.

Sometimes I just want to throw in the towel
and give up.
But I keep these words in my mind:
I am not a failure.
I am a fighter.
I am not a loser.
I am a winner.
I am not going to give up.
I am going to persevere.
In His Word it says: He won't
give us more than we can bear.

CHANGES...

So you ask me: How do I handle
the changes in my life?
This is how I handle the changes in my
life. I go into my prayer closet where I am in peace
and quiet and pray!
I handle my changes through
the Bible
and
prayer.

1 Corinthians 10:13

COUNT IT ALL JOY

Count it all joy
when things aren't
going your way.
Count it all joy
when the defeated
foe is attacking you
from the north, south,
east and west.
Count it all joy
when your friends and
family turn against you.
Count it all joy
that when you are trying
to make headway forward
you find yourself going
four steps backward.
Count it all joy;
weeping may last for the night,
but joy cometh
in the morning.
When you are under so
many attacks, watch out
and count it all joy.
Don't give up
and don't give in,
your victory is just
a step away.

So when all the tests and trials
come your way,
Remember this:
Count it all joy
and "Smile."

James 1:2-3; Psalm 30:5

COUNT ON HIM!!

 ount on Him and His Word
no matter what comes your way.
Count on all His promises.
Just have faith and believe.
Count on Him to bring you
through all the test and trials
that you are going through.
Count on Him.
He always makes a way
out of no way.
Count on Him.
He won't give to you
more than you can bear.
Count on Him.
His Word says in Matthew 7:7,
Ask, and it shall be given to you
Seek, and ye shall find
Knock, and the doors shall
and will be opened unto you.
Count on Him in
everything that you do.
Acknowledge Him, and He
will and shall direct your path.

COUNT ON HIM!!

In every decision,
In everything that you do,
In every road that you take,
In every path that you take,
In life, just do this:
Count on Him.
He will see you through.

1 Corinthians 10:13; Matthew 7:7; Proverbs 3:5-6

COVER ME

over me, Lord,
with the garment
of Your Peace.
Cover me, Lord,
with the mantle
of Your Love.
Cover me, Lord,
I ask of You today.
Cover me from all
the wiles of this world.
Cover me from all
the challenges that try
to come upon me.
Cover me, Lord,
with the mantle
of Your Love.
Cover me, Lord,
When my friends and
family forsake me,
even when the one
I took my vows with
turns his back on me.
Cover me, Lord,
with the mantle of
Your Love.

DECISIONS

Decisions that we make in life,
sometimes they are right and
sometimes they are wrong.
I have made a few bad decisions
in my life.
At times I wish I could change
the hands of time.
If I could, I would change those
bad decisions that I have made
in my life.
I often sit and wonder, if
I had done things differently,
what the outcome would have
been.
What if my decision was the
opposite of what I am doing
right now?
I often wonder
where would I be?
Would I be a happy camper
or would I be down in the
Dumpster?
I think the decisions that
we make in life,
even if they are wrong decisions,
they are learning experiences
in our lives.

This is my decision for my life:
I decide to live my life for Christ.
I decide not to be a fake.
I decide to love my brothers
and sisters to the end,
even though at times it
is so hard to do when
the same brothers and
sisters you love hurt you.
I have made these decisions for
my life.
What about you?

DISAPPOINTMENTS

e go through disappointments
in life every day, every second,
every minute, and every hour.
Sometimes we are disappointed with
our lives. Sometimes we are disappointed
with our children, and sometimes we
are disappointed with the friends that we
keep and the people that we meet.
Sometimes we are disappointed
with our spouses, and sometimes we are
disappointed with our jobs.

In everything that we do and feel as if
we are disappointed in ourselves,
remember that in every disappointment
there is an appointment. So in life we
should look at our disappointments as
being appointments in life,
appointments that we have to go
through to make us stronger in life
and with the Lord.

The meaning of disappointment: "fail to fulfill the desire or expectation of."

DO NOT GET DISCOURAGED

Do not get discouraged
when the wiles of life
get you down.

Do not get discouraged
when you thought things
were going so good and
then suddenly it goes
crashing down.

Do not get discouraged
when you are trying to
make it and you find out
that you are not.

Do not get discouraged
when you are trying to
maintain your family
and a career at the same
time and you see that things
aren't going the way that they should.

Do not get discouraged
when your child
begins to have a behavior problem
at school and at home.

Do not get discouraged
when you feel as if you
just can't take any more.
God Word says He won't give
us more than we can bear. But
you often wonder if that is true.

Do not get discouraged.
Whenever you see or feel
as if you are getting discouraged
for whatsoever reason, this is my
advice to you: go into a quiet place
and pray like you've never prayed
before, and when you are through,
shout out as loud as you can,
"Thank You, God, through Your
Son Jesus Christ, for lifting this
spirit of discouragement off me."

DO NOT JUDGE ME

Do not judge me because of the
way I look.
Do not judge me because of the
way I speak.
Do not judge me because I am
not at church every Sunday.
Do not judge me because of
my appearance.
Do not judge me because I
sin and you think you do not.
Do not judge me because I have
a baby out of wedlock.
Do not judge me because I got
pregnant at a young age.
Do not judge me because of the color
of my hair and the style I wear.
Do not judge me because my skirt
might be shorter than yours and
my shirt might be closely fitted.
Please! Please! Do not judge me.
Instead of judging me,
why don't you pray for me?
God's Word says, Judge not that
you be not judged; for with the
same measure you judge, you
will be judged.
So instead of judging each other
because of whatever reason, *Stop*!

and let us pray for each other
so that we will be judged together
by One, and that is the Great Supreme,
the King of kings
and
the Lord of lords.

Matthew 7:1-2

ENOUGH...

nough light to shine
your way through the darkness.
Enough happiness to keep
you smiling through any test and trial.
Enough trials to keep
you strong in the Lord.
Enough failure to keep
you humble.
Enough success to keep
you eager.
Enough faith to banish
all depression that tries
to come your way.
Enough friends to give
you comfort.
Enough love to conquer
any hate.
Enough determination to
make each day a better day
than yesterday.

EVEN THOUGH

ven Though you're not the
one who gave birth to me.
Even Though you're not the
one who raised me.
Even Though I've known you
for a short period of time.
Even Though you are two
in one, a confidant and a friend.
Even Though at times I do not
behave the way that I should.
Even Though at times I make
mistakes and fall on my face.
You are always there
to pray for me when
I am in need of prayer,
to listen to me when my day
is good or bad.
Your comforting words,
that soft-spoken voice of yours
saying, "Baby! Baby! You sound
tired."
Always concerned with how I feel.

Your prayers that you send
throughout the day.
Your hugs on Sunday
and your smile on Tuesday.
Your laughter when you call.

The comforting words you
speak conquer it all.
Even though all those
Even Thoughs are true,
I am blessed to have someone
like you, and I just want to say,
Thank you, and I love you...

FAITH

What is faith?
It says in His Word,
Faith is the substance
of things hoped for
and the evidence of things
not seen.
I ask myself over
and over again,
Do I have faith to
make it through the day?
Do I have faith to know
that I will see another day?
Do I have faith to
conquer the devil?
Do I have faith to bind up the defeated foe?
Do I have faith in His Word?
Do I have faith that
young men and women
will preach the gospel
and turn their lives
over to the King of kings
and the Lord of lords?
Do I have faith and
do I believe that He
will come back again one day?
Do I have faith in the
Lord Jesus Christ?
Do you have faith?

Sit, think, and ask yourself,
"Do I have faith
as a mustard seed?
Do I have the kind of faith
that can move mountains?"
What is your answer?

Hebrews 11:1; Matthew 17:20

FEAR NOT

Fear Not, when life beats you to the ground;
know that God is always around.
Fear Not, when you are fighting with the enemy;
know that He does not give up on any.
Stand strong and don't give in,
use the strength that God has placed within.

Fear Not, when your spouse approaches you with
divorce papers, and you get frantic, not knowing what
to do.
Fear Not, when the tests and trials of life try
to bring you down.

Fear Not, when your test results come back
and you receive a bad report from the doctor.

Fear Not, when your bills are past due
and you cannot see your way through.

Fear Not, when the vehicle that you are driving
decides to leave you right there on the road.

Fear Not, when things are not going right on
the job.

Fear Not, when people scandalize your name
and speak of things that you know not of.

Fear Not, when you are trying to buy a house
but your credit isn't strong enough.

Fear Not, when you find out that your spouse
is living a double life.

Fear Not, on life itself.

Fear Not, for He will never leave you, neither
will He forsake you.

Fear Not, for His Word says He will never see
the righteous forsaken or their seed begging bread.

Fear Not; if God is for you who or what can be against
you?
Why should we fear?
For God has not given us the spirit of fear.

Fear Not, for Jesus Christ died so we may
have life and have it more abundantly.
I leave you with this: Fear Not!

Hebrews 13:5; Psalm 37:25; Romans 8:31; 2 Timothy 1:7; John 10:10

FRIEND

hen someone asks me,
What is the meaning of
A friend?
This is what I tell
them:
I have a friend
who is dear to me,
besides my Lord,
he is next.

When I am down
he makes me laugh.
When I am sick
he prays for me.
When I am hungry
he brings me food.
But most of all, he's
always there for me.

This is my definition of a Friend

F—FAITHFUL
R —REAL
I—INNOCENT
E—EFFICIENT
N—NOBLE
D—DILIGENT

Yes, that's Him,
My Friend.

HAVE YOU EVER?

ave you ever felt
like you're lost and
standing all alone?

Have you ever felt
like the one you love
so much is not loving
you back?

Have you ever felt
like everything in
your life is going
upside down?

Have you ever felt
like all the problems,
tests and trials that you
are going through seem
as if they will never end?

Have you ever felt
like, where is God
when I need Him
the most? is He hearing
my prayer? and seeing my
cry?

Have you ever felt
like, I have been praying,
fasting and believing for
a breakthrough but have yet
to see a manifestation of one.

Have you ever felt
like God has forsaken
you? But His Word says,
He will never leave you,
neither will He forsake you.
But you cry out, God, where
are You? Now you think
there is no one to turn to.

Have you ever felt
like the marriage, the
relationship that you have
been working so hard on
to make it work, now it
takes a turn for the worse
and you're facing a divorce
or a separation?

Have you ever felt
like, Lord, please take
me right now out of
my misery?

Have you ever felt
all these feelings
buckled up inside
of you and you can't
wait to let it go?

What do you do now?
When all these Have You
Ever feelings are buckled up
in your heart and it starts
to ache?

Hebrews 13:5

HE IS; I HAVE

e is Mighty.
He is Great.
He moves mountains.
He conquers and devours
our enemies.
He makes our enemies
our footstool.
He gives us the key
to the kingdom.
He gives us knowledge
so we can gain wealth.
The wealth of the rich
belongs to us.
I am Rich
Not Poor.
I am Humble
Not Vain.
I am Strong
Not Weak.
I have Grace.
I have Mercy.
I have Patience.
I have The Holy Spirit
that lives inside of me.
I have the Anointing
that washes me clean.

I have the Blood of Jesus
that washes away all
my sins.
And I have the name,
the name of Jesus Christ of Nazareth.

Psalm 110:1; Matthew 16:19

HIS EYES ARE WATCHING

ook! Do you see what I see?
I feel the eyes of the Lord watching me.
I can feel it.
It is a piercing feeling.
I can feel His Eyes Watching Me.

Wrong—That is what I do not want to do.
Disobedient—That is what I am trying not to do.
I want to be obedient to Him and His Word.
Idolatry—That is a no-no for me.
Sin—Lies, deceit, adultery and stealing.
Please do keep all those away from me.
I can feel His Eyes Watching Me.

Look! Listen! Did you hear that?
Did you hear that voice?
It sounds as if He is right here
standing next to me.
I can hear it.
It is so audible.
It is getting louder.
I can hear His voice talking to me.
It sounds like the heavy beat of a drum.

Do good, and not bad.
Give, instead of trying to receive.
Love, and do not hate.
Forgive; do not live with unforgiveness
in your heart.

Trust in Me, your Heavenly Father.
Faith without works is dead.
Have faith as a mustard seed.
Listen to the voice, the voice of
the Good Shepherd.
Do them all.
It pleases Me, your Heavenly Father.

His Eyes Are Watching...

Acts 20:35; Matthew 18:21-35; James 2:17; Matthew 17:20; John 10:1-16

HIS WORD SAYS

Why do you judge me because I have a nose
ring in my nostril?
Does that make me not a child of God?
Is that considered a sin?
Does that mean I am not anointed, called and chosen?

Why do you judge me because my Heavenly Father
has blessed me with diamonds above and beyond?
Should I not be blessed with fine jewelry?
Is it a sin to wear fine jewelry that my Heavenly Father has
blessed me with?

Why do you judge me because He has anointed and
appointed
me to preach the gospel just as I am?
Should I not take His Word out to the cities and in the
fields?
His Word says: Come as you are.

Why do you judge me because of the preaching tech-
niques
that He has blessed me with? It might be different from
the
traditional way of preaching.
Should I not obey my Heavenly Father, just to please you?

Why do you judge me because of my past? My Heavenly
Father
has forgiven me of all my sins.
His Word says if I repent, He will forgive me of all my sins.

So who are you to judge me because of my past?
Why do you judge me because of my past?

Why do you judge me because my teenage daughter
has a child? So now you decide to sit and judge my house-
hold.
Who are you to judge the affairs of my household?
Don't we all make mistakes?
Don't we all sin?

Why do you judge your brother and sister when
you see them on the road?
Instead of judging them, why don't you offer
a helping hand.
Would you like your Heavenly Father to ignore
you when you are in need of help?

Why do you judge?
In the B-i-b-l-e His Word says,
Judge Not.
So why do you judge?
Stop judging your brothers and sisters.
Stop judging that teenage mother.
Stop judging the person on the corner.
Stop judging the pastors who are bringing
forth the Word. They are God's chosen vessels.
Stop judging.
We are one in Jesus Christ.
So why should we judge each other?

1 John 1:9; Romans 3:23; Matthew 7:1-2; Romans 12:5

HOW MUCH MORE?

How much more can I bear
with all this hurt and pain?
How much more can I bear
with all these lies and deceit?
How much more can I bear
with all these false pretenses?
Please tell me, Lord.
How much more can I bear?
Your Word says You won't
give us more than we can bear.
But sometimes I wonder if that
is true.
The load gets heavy and
the body gets weak.
I have been enduring a lot!
and a lot!
Please tell me, when will all
this endurance end?
What am I doing wrong?
Please tell me, Lord.
How much more can I bear?

1 Corinthians 10:13

I AM

Am Great
Even though you think
I am small.
I Am Worthy
Even though you limit
My Capability.
I Am Mighty.
Do not limit My Ability.
I Am Able and I Am Capable.
Do not look at My outward
Appearance.
I clothe My people
With garments.
Garments of Wool.
Garments of Linen.
Garments of Satin.
I Am the Maker and
I Am the Finisher.
Of all things!
Who Am I?

John 1:1-3; Hebrews 12:2

I AM HERE; ARE YOU THERE?

 am here when you call.
I AM here when you are in need.
I AM here when you are sick.
I am here when you are in need of comfort.
I am here when you are in trouble.
I am here when your friends turn their backs on you.
I am here when your mother and father forsake you.
I am here when you think you are not worthy.
I am here when you have fallen into sin.
I am here when no one else is around.
I am here when the tests and trials come upon you.
I am here when you knock.
I am here when you call My name.
Who Am I?

Are you there when I call?
Are you there when I am knocking but get no answer?
Are you there when I call you to preach the gospel?
Are you there when I instruct you to serve your pastors?
Are you there when I am tugging on your heart to change
your ways?
Who Am I?

I SURRENDER

urn it over to Him.
He knows all that we
are going through.
Surrender it all to Him.
Your spouse is acting up.
Surrender that soul over to Him.
Your children are acting up.
Surrender them over to Him.
You are having problems on the job.
Turn it all over to Him.
Your bills are due and you see no way through.
Turn it all over to Him.
You are having challenges (sickness) in your body.
Turn it all over to Him.

At times we believe that we can do it on our own.
We get headaches, fall into depression,
just simply worrying about everything.
Why should we worry or why should we
be depressed,
if we believe and trust in God through
His son Jesus Christ?
Don't you believe He can make a way out of no way?
Don't you know He can make the impossible to be possible?
Don't you know He can turn that negative situation that you
are going through into a positive one?
The doctors say this is it, they cannot help you.
Where man says, "No," God steps in and says, "Yes!"

I SURRENDER

Why depend and put your trust in man
when there is a greater one? And that is our Heavenly
Father, our Supreme Being,
the King of kings, the Lord of lords.

This is my suggestion to you:
Just surrender and say, "Yes, God, yes."

I THANK HIM

e ought to give thanks to the
Most High God.
The King Of kings
And
The Lord Of lords.
I Thank Him for waking my family
and me up every morning.
I Thank Him for the clothes on
my back and the shoes on my feet.
I Thank Him for the use of all my senses.
I Thank Him for the house that He has blessed us with.
I Thank Him for my family.
I Thank Him for my job.
I Thank Him for my loved ones.
I Thank Him for my friends.
I Thank Him for the tests and trials
that I have gone through in life.
One might say, why do I Thank Him
For the tests and trials?
This is the reason why I do:
The tests and the trials that I have gone
through in life makes me stronger and
wiser to the things that happen in my life.
So on that note, in all the fights,
In all the disappointments,
In all the hurts,

I THANK HIM

In all the failures that I go through in life,
In all the pain that I bear,
I still have to Thank Him.

I'LL SAY, "YES, LORD"

isten!...Did you hear that?
Someone is calling my name.
I hear it a second time.
A rush of thrill runs through
my body.
Did you hear that again?
Someone is calling my name
but there is no one around.
Is it who I think it is?
It is getting more audible.
It is Him...Speak to me, Lord.

*Are you willing, My child, to turn
from your sinful ways and follow
Me, your Heavenly Father?*

*Are you willing to go in the city
and in the field to bring My people
to know Me, their Heavenly Father?*

*Are you willing to bring the young,
the old, the homeless, single parents,
unwed mothers, homosexuals, drug
users, and prostitutes to know the Word
of God?*

*Are you willing to carry the mantle that
I, your Heavenly Father, have placed in your hands?*

I'LL SAY "YES LORD"

*Are you willing to do the perfect will of
Me, your Heavenly Father?*

What's your answer, My child?

Yes, Lord!
I'll say, "Yes."

I'LL WAIT...

I will wait until
the sun starts to shine.
And I'll wait
until the morning light.
And I'll wait
until He hears my cry.
I will wait.
I won't let anyone
steal my joy.
I'll wait
until I hear His voice.
I'll wait
until God calls me forth.
I'll wait
for God to ease my pain.
I'll wait
until He calls my name.
And in all my waiting
I just want to say,
Thank You, Lord.
I'll wait.
Yes!
I'll wait.

IS THIS REAL?

s this real?
This feeling that I
am feeling—
is it real?
I feel like I have
taken a trip—to
where? I ask myself.
To a place that I know
not.
It felt as if I had been
captured in another world.
Everyone looked different and spoke
with a soft-spoken voice.

So, what did you see there?
Honestly, one person spoke
to me.
What did this person say?
She had a message for her
daughter and granddaughter.
She was in a lily-white robe,
wrapped around her body.
How do you feel now?
It feels different. Like I said
before, I wonder to myself,
Is this real?

How can you experience
a feeling like this?

How can you explain a
feeling like this?
I sit and I wonder, I become
distant, I cry and cry.

Why do you cry?
Honestly, I do not know.
I just feel tears in my eyes.
I just can't explain it all.
I know I feel different, not
myself.

How different do you feel?
What do you mean by feeling
different?

Let me answer the first question. I feel
a spirit of calmness. My mind
is just not here. I am
in a little world all by
myself. Yes, I am here
at work, but my body,
mind and soul just feel
different. It feels like I
have been abducted and
my entire body went through
an out-of-body visitation.

Second question, I cannot explain it. If
I told you that I can explain how
I really feel, I would be lying.

To me, I just feel this is
a wake-up call and I have
on my mind two questions
about things that I have experience
in the past.
I just want to say, Thank You
for choosing me to be the messenger.

Just a little advice: if anyone
experienced what I have encountered
and your life is not dedicated
to God, now would be a good
time to rededicate your life
to Him. Even if you did
not encounter what I have
encountered, now would be
a good time to dedicate your
life to Christ.

Just say these words: Father,
forgive me. I am sorry. Please
help me. I come to You
broken; now please let me
be whole. I dedicate my life
to You, all of me. Now cleanse
me and wash me clean of all
unrighteousness and deliver
me from all evil. Wash me with
the blood of Jesus Christ of
Nazareth.
And by His Grace, I am now saved.
Amen.

ISN'T IT?

sn't it amazing?
How God works.
Isn't it amazing?
How He works in our lives.
Isn't it amazing?
How He makes a way
out of no way.
Isn't it amazing?
How He makes the birds
that fly in the sky.
Isn't it amazing?
The way the trees grow
and the plants bloom.
Isn't it amazing?
How He makes men and women,
boys and girls.
Isn't it amazing?
How when you are in need
He is always there to provide
right on time.
Isn't it amazing?
How He made the stars in the sky
and the sun to shine.
Isn't it amazing?
How He made the clouds in the sky
with different shapes and forms.
Isn't it amazing?

How he made the sky, the moon, the stars
and the sun that shine.
Isn't it amazing how He made them all?
Isn't it amazing?
How He hears our prayers
and answer them all.
Isn't it amazing?
How He made us all.

IT IS...

It is a lovely feeling
when you wake up
and see a new day.
It is a blessing when
you can repeat this
scripture: This is the
day that the Lord
has made and I
will rejoice and
be glad in it.
It is a miracle
when you are
a child of God
and you are
not being
tempted, tested or
tried by the
defeated foe.
It is Faith that
keeps me going
every day because
His Word says: If you
have faith as mustard seed
you can move mountains.
So it is His faith that
keeps me going through
every day.

It is because of my belief in God
through His Son Jesus Christ
that I can see the sun shining,
the wind blowing through the trees,
the clouds forming their shapes in
the sky. I can see the moon and the
stars taking up their rightful positions.
And
It is because of His Grace and Mercy
that I am here right now.
If it wasn't for His grace and mercy,
where would I be right now?
That is why in everything
that I do I have to give
thanks.
It Is because of God through
His Son Jesus Christ that I
am here today.

Psalm 118:24; Matthew 17:20; 1 Thessalonians 5:18

JESUS! CALL ON HIS NAME

hat do you do
when you have done all you can?
It seems like He is not hearing you.
You have been praying.
You have been fasting your way through.
Just call on His Name—
Jesus!

What do you do
when you find out that
your teenage daughter is pregnant?
Never thought this would happen to you.
The thought of having this to go through
brings depression and failure to your mind.
What can you do, but to call on His Name—
Jesus!

How do you handle the guilt and the shame?
To hear that one of your loved ones caught AIDS,
What can you do, but to call on His Name—
Jesus!

What do you do?
You are at work, the day is almost over,
finishing up the work that is on your
desk. Here comes your boss.
We have to talk.
Can you step into my office for a brief minute?
We need to talk. You are a hard worker.

Your job performance is excellent.
It is not you, but we have to let you go.
What can you do, but to call on His Name—
Jesus!

It is time for you to pack up and leave.
You gather all your supplies, everything
that you have collected throughout the
years, exiting the building, making your
way to the parking lot to put your things
in the car, slowly approaching your parking space,
only to see that your car is not there.
What can you do, but to call on His Name—
Jesus!

JOURNEY

The journey that we have
to take in life sometimes
makes us wonder if the journey
that we are on is really
called for.
But as we climb up that
hill and make the journey,
our bodies, minds and souls
gets weary, tired and weak.
One thing we have to remember
on our journey is that Jesus Christ
made that same journey for you and me.
So as we go through our journey
in whatsoever He ordered or called us to do,
we have to have a mind like Christ
and climb the ladder and go through
the journey just like He did.
And through the journey
we have to remember to ask
Him for Grace and Mercy.
And as our bodies get
weary, tired, and weak,
we have to remember this:
We can do all things through
Christ who strengthens us
and
We are more than conquerors.
Sometimes, even when the journey

gets harder and it seems as if we
are not getting to our destination,
we still have to stand strong and persevere.
We have to be persistent in this journey that
we are on.
We cannot give up now,
because He has placed us
on this journey.

Philippians 4:13; Romans 8:37

JUST A LITTLE OF YOUR TIME

Are you so busy that a little
of your time cannot be spared?
A little of your time is all He needs.
Just a little of your time to pray.
Just a little of your time to worship.
Just a little of your time to fast.
Just a little of your time to seek His face.
Just a little time to receive Him.
Just a little of your time is all He needs.

Are you so busy that you cannot
worship Him?
Are you so busy that you cannot pray?
Are you so busy that you cannot seek
His face or receive Him?
Are you really that busy?

What if He were too busy to hear
all of your prayers?
What if He were too busy to wipe away
all those tears?
What if He were too busy to erase
all your hurt and pain?
What if He were too busy to hear your call?
What if He were too busy to protect you
from all incidents and accidents?
What if He were too busy to wake you up
this morning?
What if He were too busy when you are

trying to explain the things that you did
and asking for His forgiveness?
Sit and think on these things.

Just a little of your time is all He needs.
So instead of being too busy on the phone
or driving here and there, spend a little time
with Him. He is worth it.
Just a little of your time is all He needs.

LIFE

ife is what you make it.
Sometimes you're up
and
sometimes you're down.
Sometimes you don't even
know if you are up or down.
One thing I know, if you are
up or down, you have to give
God thanks for life.
Someone went to bed last night and
did not know that was their last
night to see their loved ones,
to speak to their sister or brother
or to see their mother and father,
even to hear their son and daughter
say, I love you!
Life is what you make it.
So be cautious and live your
life for Christ.
These are my four words for life:

L is for Live
I is for In
F is for Forever
E is for Eternity

Live In Forever Eternity.

LITTLE DO THEY KNOW

ittle do they know who I am.
Little do they know that I was sent here for such a time as this.
Little do they know that if God is for me, who or what can be against me?
Little do they know that many are called but few are chosen.
Little do they know that God has made me the head and not the tail.
Little do they know that I am more than a conqueror through Christ Jesus.
Little do they know that I can do all things through Christ who strengthens me.
Little do they know that the wealth of the sinner is laid up for the just.
Little do they know that the Lord is my shepherd, I shall not want.
Little do they know that I fight not against flesh and blood but against principalities and powers in high places.
Little do they know that what God has for me, it is for me.
Little do they know that He has given me authority to use the blood and the name of Jesus Christ.
Little do they know that faith that without works is dead.
Little do they know that if I have faith as a mustard seed I can move all mountains.
Little do they know that He will never leave me nor forsake me.
Little do they know that I am saved by grace.

Little do they know that God blessed me with all gifts.
Little do they know that I am a prophet of God.
Little do they know!

Esther 4:14; Romans 8:31; Matthew 22:14; Deuteronomy 28:13; Romans 8:37; Philippians 4:13; Proverbs 13:22; Psalm 23:1; Ephesians 6:12; James 2:17; Matthew 17:20; Hebrews 13:5; Ephesians 2:8; Ephesians 1:3

LOOK AT ME

ook at me, a mother of two,
        one boy, one girl.
Working hard from Monday to Friday
and sometimes on Saturday.

Working hard to make ends
meet. Working hard to put food
on the table so they can eat.

Teaching them it is better to do
good than bad. Teaching them that
life is a learning experience and
never say never, because you
never know what the future holds.
Instead of saying never, just say
these words: I pray to God that I will
never do whatsoever I am saying never to,
and He will bring you through.

LOST IN DESPAIR

e are broken and lost in despair.
The soul has gone away and is lost in despair.
Why don't you let go and walk on in?
The soul has lost and gone in despair.
We sit and look as if we are all right inside.
The layer outside is so torn in my eyes.
Who do you think you are impressing?
When you are lost in my sight.

The soul is lost and gone in despair.
Why don't you let it go and walk on in?
Sitting and looking around to see who
might have known.
Wondering when, oh Lord.
I know You've heard my cry.
I know You've seen my hurt and pain deep
down inside.

I kept on praying.
I kept on believing.
I kept on trusting.
My soul has gone and
I am lost in despair.
Can you please help me, Lord,
from all this pain?
It is hurting so deep inside
and I am lost in despair.

"LOST IN DESPAIR"

Can you lift this hurt
that I am feeling inside?
My soul has gone away and
I am lost in despair.

MY CHILDREN

Sometimes I have to scold you guys
when you are getting out of line.
Sometimes I just have to love you guys,
so that you both will know how
much I love you.
At times when I am feeling down, that
is when you both try to act like clowns.
Even though I scold and reprimand you
both, I just want you guys to know that I
still love you.
In His Word it says: Do not spare the rod
and spoil the child. Whenever that young
one needs to be disciplined and you feel
guilty in doing so, go to His Word and it
will show you that we are responsible for
that soul.

Proverbs 13:24

79

MY DAUGHTER

One day my daughter will see and experience
all that I was trying to instill in her. She has a
baby boy now, and I know that she will remember
all the things that I have tried to teach her. All the
wrongs from the right. All the doing good instead of evil,
and all the teaching about the Word and what she needs
to do to please God.
I pray that she will instill it all in my grandson's life. She
is a good kid, you know. Always in her books, trying to
make
the grades, and most of all trying to be in the right
standing with
her Heavenly Father. I love my daughter dearly, and I just
want
the best for her and my grandson.

MY SON

I pray that I will live to see my son with his family coming over to visit me. He is a special little boy, so dear and close to my heart. That's my premature baby, trying to enter in before his time. I pray that all that I have taught him, he will not forget and in turn will do the same for his child. I try to instill in him the right way I know how and to pray at all times and never forget to tell God through His Son Jesus Christ, Thank You.
I love my son dearly. I just want the best for him.

1 Thessalonians 5:17

MY GRANDSON

That is my little angel. A blessing and miracle that was sent to me. He is always running around trying to get himself in some kind of trouble. His name is always shouted out in the living room, in the family room or in the bedroom. He is always messing with something that does not belong to him. He is a joy to have. I love my grandson dearly and I pray blessings over his life.

In life at times we have to show appreciation before it's too late, even by making a homemade card to express how you feel. A phone call will do too, just to say I love you. Do not wait until it's too late to show someone how much you appreciate them and how close they are to your heart. Never put off what you can do today for tomorrow, because you can never tell what tomorrow holds.

Proverbs 27:1; James 4:14

MY DAY

don't know
how I feel right now.
The day is gloomy.
My mind is racing
like horses in the field,
a lot of thoughts going
through my mind.
Should I go there? Or,
Should I stay here?
A lot of signs going
across my head.
Wondering what should
I do next.
As the day progresses,
I will see what kind
of day this will be for me.
I can make my day good
or I can make my day bad.
I can make it a joyous day
or I can make it sad.
I can repeat these words
in my mind: This is the day
that the Lord has made and
I will rejoice and be glad
in it.
It all narrows down
to me.

MY DAY

How do I want my
day to be?
Even though circumstances
and situations might try to
get me down,
I still have to thank God
that He is always there
with me.

Psalm 118:24

MY GRAND-MOMMY

ords cannot express the way how I
feel about my Grand-Mommy.
She has done so much for me.
She is always there when I need her,
even when I don't.
My Grand-Mommy is a Sweet, Loving
Caring, Nurturing and Dynamic Woman
who believes in God.
She always gives me encouraging words to
help me on my way.
My Grand-Mommy has always been there
for me in good times and bad times.
Giving me advice, protecting me in any way
she can.
She never puts me down, even when I am wrong.
Words cannot express the things that my Grand-
Mommy has done for me.
She is a friend when I need a friend.
She doctors me when I am sick.
She comforts me when I need to be comforted.
She is an adviser when I need advice.
She is My Grand-Mommy, that's what she is,
and
I am blessed to have a Grand-Mommy like the one
that I have, and I love her with all my heart and with
every bone that's in my body.
That is how much my Grand-Mommy means to me.

NEVER GIVE UP!

ever give up
when things are not
going your way.
Never give up
when you are trying
to pay the bills and your
money comes up short.
Never give up
when you are going through
test and trials and it seems
as if it is not going to end.
Never give up
when you have been
crying out His name and
you see no change.
Never give up
when your children
start to act up at school
and at home and you are
wondering, Why, Lord?
Never give up
when the one you love
so much turns away
from you.
Never give up
even when your own
family members forsake
you.

Never give up
when you find out
that one of your beloved
family members is on
drugs and another one
is dying of AIDS.
Never give up
when it looks like
everyone is making it
but you.
Never give up.
Just continue to trust
in and on your Heavenly
Father, because His Word
says He will never leave
you, neither will He forsake
you.
So knowing all that,
you can now say this:
"I Will Never Give Up!"

Hebrews 13:5

NO MORE TEARS!

o More Tears.
That is what I say
to myself.
No More Tears!
I have been beating
upon myself.
For what? I ask myself.
For things that happened
in the past.
For things I wish would
not have taken place.
The tears of sorrow so
overwhelming.
My heart is full of pain.
It is time for me to say:
No More Tears!
I know I cannot turn back
the hands of time.
I know what is done is done.
But still I sit and look into all
that I have been through, still
crying deep inside,
wondering, When will it all end?
Is this a dream or is it reality?
That is when the Lord answered
me and said these words:
No More Tears!

PLEASE HELP ME

Please help me to do good and
not bad.
Please help me to live righteous and
not unrighteous.
Please help to love and
not to hate.
Please help me to obey and
not to disobey.
Please help me to live holy and
not unholy.
Please help me to do right and
not wrong.
Please help me to be a leader and
not a follower.
Please help me to walk the walk and
talk the talk like Christ.
Please help me to forgive others
like Christ forgives us.
Please help me.
This walk is not easy and
the road seems longer, but as we take
this walk it gets harder.
Remember, don't give up,
just turn to Him and say
these four words:
Lord, please help me!

PRAYING & FASTING

What are you praying and fasting for?
Are you praying and fasting for a job?

Are you praying and fasting for a new home?

Are you praying and fasting for a husband
or a wife?

Are you praying and fasting for a better relationship
with your spouse?

Are you praying and fasting for a better understanding
with your children?

Are you praying and fasting for a closer relationship
with God?

Are you praying and fasting for wisdom, knowledge,
understanding, guidance, favor and honor, grace and
mercy
with God?

Are you praying and fasting for an increase,
not only financially, but also spiritually and mentally?

Are you praying and fasting for strength and
the ability to cope with the world that we live in?

Are you praying and fasting for the children and
this society that we live in?

Are you praying and fasting to bind up the defeated foe
from our young men and women?

Are you praying and fasting for our young men
to stop crime on crime?

Are you praying and fasting for our young ladies
with teenage pregnancies, disease and unwed parenting?

Are you praying and fasting to stop the rate of divorce?

Are you praying and fasting that men, women, children
and babies will seek our Heavenly Father?

Are you praying and fasting for the children
and this FCAT?*

Are you praying and fasting for a promotion
on your job and an increase in salary?

Are you really praying and fasting, or
are you just looking and watching?

What are you doing?

Instead of looking and watching, let's take three to seven
of the praying and fasting requests that are listed above,
and let's really pray and fast on these things.

*Florida Comprehensive Assessment Test

PURPOSE

have a purpose.
What is the meaning of *purpose?*
Purpose: 1. Design; end or aim
desired. 2. object kept in view;
determination.
There are several meanings
of *purpose*, which one will
you choose?

I have a purpose: to live
and not to die.
I have a purpose: to do good
and not bad.
I have a purpose: to do right
and not wrong.
I have a purpose: to win
and not to lose.
I have a purpose: to make it
and not to fail.
I have a purpose: to move speedily
and not to slumber.
I have a purpose: to love
and not to hate.
I have a purpose: to live in light
and not in darkness.
I have a purpose: to live my
life for Christ
and not for the devil.

I have a purpose: Thus Saith
The Lord.
I have a purpose for my life,
Do you?

QUENCH ME, LORD

Quench me, Lord.
Not only with Your
love.
Not only with Your
comfort.
Not only with Your
Spirit.
Quench me, Lord.
Quench me with Your
forgiveness.
Quench me with your
peace.
Quench me with Your
loving-kindness.
Quench me with Your
grace and mercy.
Quench me with favor
and honor with You, Lord.
Quench me, Lord.
There are times that I am
thirsty, not for water or juice
but for You, Lord.
Quench me with Your
Word.
Quench me with Your
direction.
I need You to
Quench me, Lord.

REALITY

hat is Reality?
What is the meaning of Reality?
Let us start with, what is Reality?

Reality is when your daughter
comes home and says, "Mommy, I'm
in love with someone you are not really
fond of."

Reality is when almost everyone on your
job is being promoted, with the exception
of you.

Reality is to find out that the mate that you
thought was being so loyal and faithful,
now you find out that he or she is living a
double life.

Reality is when your husband or wife comes
home and says, "I don't think this is going
to work out. Can I have a divorce?"

Reality is when your teenage daughter
comes to you and says, "Mommy, we have to
talk. Please don't be disappointed in me when
I am through talking to you. Mommy, I am
pregnant."

Reality is when our young men and boys are
selling drugs and doing this crime on crime,
shooting and looting. And our young women
and girls are stealing and prostituting.

Reality is when your light bill, water bill
and your rent or mortgage is due, but you don't
see your way through.
Let us now look at the meaning of *Reality*:

1. What is real or existent or underlies appearance
2. The real nature (of)
3. Real existence; state of being real
4. In reality; in fact

This is my meaning of Reality: Reality to me is my
everyday
life, things and situations that really take place in my life.

That is
Reality to me.

SACRIFICE

1. What sacrifice are you willing to make for Jesus Christ?
2. Are you willing to make a sacrifice to follow Christ?
3. Are you willing to make a sacrifice to be like Christ?
4. Are you willing to give up all your sinful ways to follow Christ?
5. Are you willing to go on the highways and corners to win souls for Christ?
6. Are you willing to sacrifice yourself to do the perfect will of Christ?
7. Are you willing to sacrifice your children for Christ if He tells you to?
8. Are you willing to sacrifice all your worldly possessions for Christ?
9. Are you willing to sacrifice that good novel and pick up His Word and study?
10. Are you willing to sacrifice for Jesus Christ?
11. Are you willing to sacrifice your life for Christ?
12. Are you willing to sacrifice it all for Christ?

Think on these twelve questions, and really search your soul, and answer with honesty and sincerity of the heart. Are you willing and ready to sacrifice one, if not all, at least half, for your savior, Jesus Christ?

SIT BACK AND WATCH GOD

hen troubles and trials try to bring you down,
do not get frustrated and do not get weary.
Just Sit Back and Watch God.

Looking at your paycheck wondering how ends
are going to meet, putting in all the hours, minutes,
and seconds. Here comes payday, and you are
disappointed when you see your paycheck.
Do not get frustrated and do not get weary.
Just Sit Back and Watch God.

Challenges of life have you wondering,
When will all this come to an end?
Don't know where to turn.
Don't know who to run to.
Looking and waiting for all this to
come to an end.
Do not get frustrated and do not get weary.
Just Sit Back and Watch God.

You are on your way to work and your car
starts acting up. The time is going.
You are praying your way through, and during
your prayer the car stops—Dead!
Worried and frustrated, wondering what you are going to
do.
Now you are late for work and your boss is going to
have a nervous breakdown.
"The presentation is in the car. What am I going to do?"

Do not get frustrated and do not get weary.
Just Sit Back and Watch God.

You are doing everything you can
to make your marriage work. Cleaning
the house, making sure the children's homework gets done,
and in bed. Having dinner prepared, waiting for your hus-
band to
get home. As the time goes by, ticktock, still waiting to
hear the
keys open the door. You waited so long you got tired of
waiting
so you place the food in the microwave and turn off the
lights,
upset and frustrated about it all.
Do not get frustrated and do not get weary.
Just Sit Back and Watch God.

In everything that you do
acknowledge Him and He
will direct your path.
When the troubles and trials
try to get you down,
Just Sit Back and Watch God
Move!

Proverbs 3:5-6

SO WHAT?

So what! I got pregnant at a young age.
So what! My car got repossessed.
So what! I have piercings all over my body.
So what! My coworkers talk about me and slander my
name.
So what! My family members turn their backs on me.
So what! I lost my job and now I am on public assistance.
So what! I was incarcerated and on death row.
So what! The church folks look at me and turn up their
noses when they see me.
So what! I have a disability and no one would know.
So what! My mother tried to kill this seed.

I say "so what" because God through His Son
Jesus Christ forgave me of that sin of fornication.
I say "so what" because His Word says "come as you
are."
I say "so what" because they slandered Jesus too.
I say "so what" because Jesus Christ is a rewarder
of those who diligently seek Him.
I say "so what" because He has been a provider
for all my needs.
I say "so what" because His Word says "do not judge."
I say "so what" because God through His Son Jesus
Christ can heal all sickness and disease.

1 John 1:9; Hebrews 11:6; Matthew 7:1-2.

SPEAK TO ME

Speak To Me, Lord.
I need to hear from You.
There are so many things
that have been going on.
Speak To Me, Lord.
I need to hear from You.
I need You to show me which
direction I should go.
Speak To Me, Lord.
I need to hear from You.
I have a lot of questions on
my mind that I need answers to.
Speak To Me, Lord.
I need to hear from You.
I have been tried.
I have been tested.
I have been going through
trials and tribulations.
When will all this end?
Speak To Me, Lord.
I need to hear from You.

What do you do when
you can't hear from Him?
What do you do when
you are calling on Him but
He is not responding?
Tell me, what do you do?

What do you do when
you need to speak to Him?
Just one word, I
ask from You, Lord.
Speak To Me, Lord.
I need to hear from You.

STRUGGLES

I am a strong woman
who goes through a lot
of struggles in life.
I am not talking about you,
but I am speaking for myself.
Yes, myself!
I have struggles with my children
to do the right and not the wrong.
They say I talk a lot.
Yes, I might talk a lot, that is what
they say.
But do they listen?
"No!"
I say they don't.
I have struggles on the job.
Trying to get the work done
that has been assigned to me.
The supervisor is telling me
to do it one way.
Then here comes the manager,
telling me to do it another way.
So then what happens?
I get stuck in the middle, trying
to figure out which way I can
do this and get it done correctly.
Confusion tries to sneak its way in.
But No! No! No! I say.

STRUGGLES

I sit, pray and ask God for His
guidance and direction how to get
it done correctly.
There are a lot of struggles in life.
But we have to remember this:
We cannot let the struggles of life
get us down.
We have to stand strong, have faith,
believe and fight all these
Struggles
of Life.

TAKE A LOOK WITHIN YOURSELF

t is time for us to be real with ourselves.
We need to stop the talking and backbiting.
Let's stop all of the gossiping.
And you call yourself a child of God.

Do you think children of God should talk
against each other?
Take a look within yourself.
Are you an example of a child of God?

Yes, that's what you say, but yet you see
your sister or brother in pain and you turn
and walk away with not a bit of concern with
why they are in pain.

How can you walk away from your sister or brother
when they are in pain?
Take a look within yourself.
Is that an action of a child of God?
What Would Jesus Do?
Would He have walked away, seeing that one of us
is in pain?

How can you say that you love the Father,
but yet your brother and sister are facing
you each and every day here on earth are in pain, and you
turn your back and walk away.

Backbiting, Gossiping, Hypocrisy, Hurt and Pain
do not come from our Heavenly Father.
So when we see our sister or brother in pain, please!
please! do not walk away.
And when the enemy brings gossiping lips, backbiting
spirits and hypocrisy against our sisters and brothers,
give the enemy notice and do not entertain that spirit.
Just keep saying this: I am a child of God, and what would
Jesus do?
Really take a look within yourself.
It is time to do a soul search.
Are your actions pleasing to God through His Son Jesus
Christ?

THANK HIM

What more can I say
but thank You,
Lord, for all You have done
and about to do in and through
our lives.
I just want to thank Him
from the smallest to the
largest thing that He has
done in my life.
We might sit and think
we are worse off than the
man next door,
only to find out that the
man next door does not
have any light, water or
money to buy food.
Really think on this and
let me know if God has ever
left you or forsaken you.
Think on these, and really
meditate on them.
Answer them within yourself:

1.   Do you have a roof over your head?
2.   Do you have a bed to sleep on?
3.   Do you have food and the essentials?
4.   Do you have light and water in your
place of residence?

5.   Are your children alive and well?

6.   Do you have a job?

If five of your answers are "Yes" and one is "No,"
That should be enough to thank Him, and
you can say this much:
God never leaves me
and
God never forsakes me.

Hebrews 13:5

THE LIGHT

One might ask What is The Light?
The Light is the Holy Spirit that is in you.
The Light is the Anointing that He places on you.
The Light is the Blood that He shed just for you.
Let the Light shine that is in you.

His Word says, "If you are not ashamed of Me,
Then I won't be ashamed of you."
Why should you be ashamed of the one who
died on the cross for us?
The one who took the nails in His hands.
The one who took the stripes on His back.
The one who had the thorns on His head.
The one who was hanged for you and me.
The one who was between a thief and a murderer.
The one whose blood was shed for you and me.
Why should we be ashamed of the King of kings
and the Lord of lords?

Put yourself in that position; really think about it:
Would you have done that?
Would you have taken the nails in your hands?
Would you have taken those stripes on your back?
How would you feel to have thorns on your head?
How would you like to be hung? Think about it;
How would you feel?
Would you like to be between a thief and a murderer
When you know you are innocent?

Tell me, why should we be ashamed of Him?
I can boldly say I am sold out for Jesus Christ.
Can you?

Mark 8:38

THE LORD IS MY SHEPHERD

PLEASE PLACE THE NAME OF THE PERSON
IN THE BLANK SPACES.

The Lord is _____**'s shepherd**

_____ shall not want.

He maketh _____ to lie down

in green pastures: He leadeth _____

beside the still waters.

He restoreth _____'s soul: He leadeth

_____ in the path of righteousness for

His name's sake.

Yea though _____ walk through the

valley of the shadow of death.

_____ will fear no evil: for thou art

with _____: thy rod and thy staff they

comfort _____.

Thou preparest a table before _____

in

the presence of _____'s enemies: thou

anointest _____'s head with oil:

_____ cup runneth over.

Surely goodness and mercy shall follow

_____ all the days of _____'s

life: and _____ will dwell in the house

of the Lord forever.

THE REFLECTION

ook in the mirror,
What do you see?
The reflection of you,
Looking back at you.
Do you like what you see?
Are you pleased with the reflection that you see?

There comes a time in life when we have to change.
We cannot always live that messed-up way.
If the reflection that you see is not pleasing to you,
I think it is time for you to do something new.
Go on your knees and pray to God
for Him to change you from within.
Life is not promised to you or me.
It is time for us to get ourselves together.
It is time for us to fall on our knees.
It is time for us to change the reflection of what we see.

The reflection reflects our lives, you see.
Let us give a good reflection so that God will be pleased.
Let's start today to change our ways.
Fall on our knees and pray.
Ask Him to guide us in the right way,
Provide us with wisdom and knowledge as we pray.

Let the reflection of Jesus Christ shine
through You, and let it be so bright
that everyone can see the *reflection* of
God in you.

THE SUNSHINE

very morning when you wake up
look into the mirror and say these words:
I am a beautiful person who is full with
the Grace and Mercy of God.
I am filled with the sunshine that shines through out
the day.
I am filled with His Spirit that takes me through the day.
I am filled with the Word that carries me along the way.
I am a beautiful sunshine, that is what He says.

So if your friends or family members tells you different,
Just look at them and say, I am a beautiful sunshine for
Jesus and that is all that matters.
You can also tell them that you have a little info for them.
They can also be a sunshine for Jesus if they choose to
change their ways.

THE TABERNACLE OF THE LORD

ake me to Your tabernacle.
Take me so I can find rest.
There is peace in your tabernacle.
The tabernacle of the Lord
is where I want to be.

What is the meaning of tabernacle?
"Temporary dwelling place of the soul."

Wouldn't you like to go into the tabernacle
of the Lord with me?
In the tabernacle
you will find Love.
In the tabernacle of the Lord,
that's where I want to be.
Take me, Lord,
into your tabernacle.
I need peace
I need love
I need joy
I need rest
I need to be in the tabernacle
of the Lord.

THE VESSEL

This vessel that I have belongs
To my *Heavenly Father.*
This vessel is in need of His direction
and guidance for my life.
This vessel want to do the
perfect will of *God.*
This vessel wants to walk in the
victory of *God.*
This vessel wants the knowledge
and wisdom of *God.*
This vessel wants to minister the
Word of *God.*
This vessel is fully sold out to *God*
through His Son *Jesus Christ.*
This vessel has been delivered from
bondage by the grace of *God.*
This vessel has been healed by the
Blood of God.
This vessel has been truly anointed
by *God.*
This vessel walks by faith through
the love of *God.*
This vessel has the peace of *God.*
This vessel has been blessed by *God.*
This vessel has the glory and victory
through *God.*

THE VESSEL

This vessel has the courage and boldness
to profess that *God* through His Son *Jesus Christ* is my
Lord and Savior.
This vessel has been delivered from fear
with the help of *God.*
This vessel has no doubt, because of the
mercy of *God.*

This vessel really and truly belongs to
the Trinity and is sold out to God the Father, Jesus Christ
the Son, and the Holy Spirit.

TRUST

Trust. What is trust?
We often hear this: Trust in God
and lean not on your own under-
standing.
Sometimes it is so hard to have that
trust when the bills, the job, the children,
sickness and the pay rate are all coming
down on you at once.

Have you ever worked all week and here comes
payday, and when you receive your check you
are so disappointed to see what your income is?
Then you sit and think, How am I going to do this?
Where am I going to get the rest to make up the difference?
In reality, your income is way less than your outgoing bills.
So what do you do?
You sit and think about how you are going to make ends
meet.
At that point of time, you are not thinking about trust.
You are calculating here and there, not knowing how it is
going
to be done, not knowing if you should trust in the Lord.
He is right there, waiting to hear from you.
He may not come when you want Him, but He will be
there right on time.

Have you ever been in a position where you are really in
need of a financial breakthrough, and all you are doing is
praying and trusting that God will bring you through? You

are at your wits' end, and there He goes, just shows up
and out, right in time. Oh! You have never been there, so
I guess you have never been in that position where your
light, water, phone, cable, rent and daycare are due all at
the same time and you have no means of paying them all.
Well, I have been there, and I know who brought me
through.
I know about trusting in God.
He is the only way out, especially
when you are in a tight position and
you have no one to turn to.
He is a provider when you are in need.
Trust in God and not in man.

Proverbs 3:5

WHAT'S HIS NAME? JESUS!

What's His Name?
His Name is Jesus.
Let me tell you
about that Name.
That Name is powerful.
That Name is mighty.
That Name chases demons.
That Name delivers the righteous.

What's His Name?
His name is Jesus.
Do you know Him?
If not, get to know Him.
He is a lawyer
when you are in trouble.
He is a doctor
when you are sick.
He is a comforter
when you need to be comforted.
He is a friend
when others forsake you.
He is a deliverer
when you need deliverance.

What's His Name?
His name is Jesus.
Do you know Him?
If not, get to know Him.
He will bring you joy

when you are sad.
He will bring happiness
when you are unhappy.
He will bring peace
to the peaceless mind.
He will lift all the trouble
from your troubled soul.
He will forgive you
when others will not.

What's His Name?
His name is Jesus.
Do you know Him?
If not, get to know Him.

WHAT DO YOU DO?

hat do you do?
When you are trying
to make it as a woman
or man of God and all
the wiles of this world
come at you.
And even though you
are trying your best,
everything that you do
or say, you make God
lead the way.
Nevertheless, it seems as if the more
you try, the more you are tested along
the way.
What do you do?
When you are trying so hard
with your children but
it seems as if everything that
you do turns into pain.
What do you do?
When you find out your teenage
daughter you look at as
your angel, the gem of your eyes,
is no longer a virgin.
What do you do?
When everything tries
to come against you
all at once:

WHAT DO YOU DO?

The children.
The car acting up.
The job.
The husband/wife.
The school, and your education.
No family member to turn to.

What do you do?
When everyone thinks
you have it all together
and they really do not know
all that you are carrying and dealing
with inside.
Every second, every minute,
every hour, every day it is
something new.
What do you really do?
When all these tests and trials
come against you.
What Do You Do?

WHAT IF?

hat If you had a critical disease
that the doctor cannot cure?
What would you do and
who would you turn to?

What If you are about to lose
your house and you have tried
everything in the book to keep
your home?
What would you do and
who would you turn to?

What If the only means of
transportation that you have is
being repossessed and you do
not have any way to get around?
The bus will not do and taking
a taxi will be too costly.
What would you do and
who would you turn to?

What If the job that you have
for years and years—you would
not expect with all those years
you have invested that you are
now being laid off. The company
that you thought was doing so
well now has to subside, and
unfortunately you are amongst the

ones they have to let go.
What would you do and
who would you turn to?

What If the Lord finally blessed your womb
and you are now pregnant with the bundle
of joy that you always wanted? So excited
that you are finally going to give birth to
a child of your own, so happy that you went
and bought all your baby supplies and have them
all stacked up waiting for the grand finale,
the day that you will hear the voice of that
bundle of joy crying out. You are now in your
ninth month, and it is time for you to give birth.
You give birth only to find out that unfortunately
the child is stillborn. The umbilical cord
wrapped around the baby's neck, and now your
bundle of joy is gone, dead. Now your joy turns
into sorrow, and you are now down and depressed.
What would you do and
who would you turn to?

What If all those What Ifs
came to you all at once?
Really, tell me:
What would you do and
who would you turn to?

WHEN, GOD, WHEN?

We look, sit and wonder,
When, God, when?
I have been praying.
I have been fasting.
I have been faithful.
I have been loyal.
So tell me,
When, God, when?

My light bill is due.
My rent is past due.
I am about to be
evicted anytime soon.
I look and wonder
and ask God,
When, God, when?
Bills past due.
My child needs
a new pair of shoes.
No money to spare.
All this I have to bear.
I sit, look and wonder,
When, God, when?

WHEN WAS THE LAST TIME?

When was the last time
you went before the Lord
and really thanked Him for
all that He has done and
is about to do?

When was the last time
you took up your Bible
and really read it with understanding?

When was the last time
you went into His presence and sincerely
sought His name and His face like you should?

When was the last time
you went in prayer, interceding, fasting
and believing that He can do it, He can
make the impossible possible?

When was the last time
you heard His voice and
felt His presence?

When was the last time
you practiced your mustard
seed faith? Instead of sitting
and crying that you can't,
get up, rise up and show the
devil that you can do all things
through Christ who strengthens you.

When was the last time
you really worshiped Him
like you should?

When was the last time?
Think about it, and answer
this question:
When was the last time?

Philippians 4:13

WHY ME?

As the tears
roll out of my eyes,
my heart is filled
with sorrow
and with regrets.
Thinking, where
did I go wrong?
Wondering, if I
would have done
it different,
what the outcome
would have been.
I sit and wonder,
asking God, "Why me?"
"What have I done
to deserve this
kind of treatment?"
All kind of questions
going through my mind.
All the deceit.
All the lies.
All the hurt.
All the pain.
Was it really called for?
Why me, Lord?
I keep on asking myself,
"Why me?"

WHY? OH! WHY?

am human.
I do get weary.
I do get tired.
And at times I feel
as if I am standing all alone.
I ask myself, Why? Oh! Why?
Did God hear my prayers?
Does God see my weariness?
Does God see my lonely nights
and days? Why? Oh! Why do
I feel this way?
Is it because I am not praying
hard enough?
What am I doing wrong?
Can you tell me? Why? Oh! Why do
I feel this way?
We sit in a glass house looking out,
not seeing what is going wrong.
Until suddenly! A tragedy hits
and it is facing us, face to face.
Not seeing the signs and not
recognizing the problems
and tragedy that's facing us day to day.
That is when we stop and realize
the problems and tragedy that tries
to attack us from day to day.

WHY OH!!! WHY

What do we do now, and how
do we handle it?
We sit and ponder and ask ourselves,
Why? Oh! Why?

WIPE THE TEARS AWAY

Wipe the tears away.
Why are you sitting
and lamenting over
things of the past?
Answer this one question:
Can you change or turn back
whatsoever happened in the past?
No!
Pick up your head and
wipe your tears away.
God forgives us of all our sins.
So why do we sit in the corner
and have a pity party for ourselves?

If the King of kings
and
the Lord of lords forgives us,
why shouldn't we forgive ourselves?
Let's stop and really look into ourselves
and see if all the pity parties and the tears
are really called for.

Let's stop!
Pick up our heads and
wipe the tears away.

CLOSING PRAYER

ur Father which art in heaven, Hallowed
be thy name.
Thy kingdom come. Thy will be done in
earth, as it is in heaven.
Give us this day our daily bread.
And forgive us our debts, as we forgive
our debtors.
And lead us not into temptation, but deliver
us from evil:
For thine is the kingdom, and the power, and
the glory, forever.
AMEN.

Matthew 6:9-13

Scripture Reference

Notes

Place your Prayer Request below

Place your Prayer Request below

Place your Praise Report below

_____
_____
_____
_____
_____
_____
_____
_____
_____
_____
_____
_____
_____
_____
_____
_____
_____
_____
_____
_____
_____
_____
_____
_____

Place your Praise Report below

_____
_____
_____
_____
_____
_____
_____
_____
_____
_____
_____
_____
_____
_____
_____
_____
_____
_____
_____
_____
_____
_____
_____

CLOSING SCRIPTURES

Matthew 7:1-2: *Judge not that ye be not judged for with the what judgement ye judge ye shall be judged: and with what measure ye mete, it shall be measured to you again.*

Proverbs 18:24: *A man that hath friends must shew himself friendly and there is a friend that sticketh closer than a brother.*

1st Thessalonians 5:23: *And the very God of peace sanctify you wholly; and I pray God your whole spirit and soul and body be preserved blameless unto the coming of our Lord Jesus Christ.*

Romans 8:28: *And we know that all things work together for good to them that love God, to them who are called according to his purpose.*

Hebrews 4:14: *Seeing then that we have a great high priest that is passed into the heavens, Jesus the Son God, let us hold fast our profession.*

Psalm 15:1: *Lord, who shall abide in thy tabernacle? Who shall dwell in thy holy hill?*

Proverbs 27:1: *Boast not thyself of to morrow; for thou knowest what a day may bring forth.*

Mark 11: 22-23: *And Jesus answering saith unto them, Have faith in God. For verily I say unto you that whosoever shall say unto this mountain be thou removed, and be thou cast into the sea and shall not doubt in his heart, but shall believe that those things, which he saith, shall come to pass; he shall have whatsoever he saith.*

Mark 11:24: *Therefore I say unto you, whatsoever things ye desire when ye pray, believe that ye receive them and ye shall have them.*

Ephesians 5:20: *Giving thanks always for all things unto God and the Father in the name of our Lord Jesus Christ.*

Psalm 124:8: *Our help is in the name of the Lord, who made heaven and earth.*

Matthew 6:16-17: *Moreover when ye fast be not as the hypocrites, of a sad countenance: for they disfigure their faces that they may appear unto men to fast. Verily I say unto you they have their reward. But thou, when thou fastest anoint thine head and wash thy face.*

James 5:16: *Confess your faults one to another and pray one for another that ye may be healed. The effectual fervent prayer of a righteous man availeth much.*